W9-CMS-203

CREATURES ALL AROUND US
It's a Mouse!

by D.M. Souza

Carolrhoda Books, Inc./Minneapolis

12/98
B4T

J
599.35
S

Copyright © 1998 by Carolrhoda Books, Inc.

All rights reserved. International copyright secured. No part of this book may be reproduced, stored in a retrieval system, or transmitted in any form or by any means, electronic, mechanical, photocopying, recording, or otherwise, without the prior written permission of Carolrhoda Books, Inc., except for the inclusion of brief quotations in an acknowledged review.

Carolrhoda Books, Inc., c/o The Lerner Publishing Group
241 First Avenue North, Minneapolis, MN 55401 U.S.A.
Website address: www.lernerbooks.com

Library of Congress Cataloging-in-Publication Data

Souza, D. M. (Dorothy M.)
    It's a mouse! / by D. M. Souza.
        p.   cm. – (Creatures all around us)
    Includes index.
    Summary: Describes the life cycle, characteristics, and habitats of various species of mice.
    ISBN 1-57505-087-0
    1. Mice—Juvenile literature. [1. Mice.] I. Title.
II. Series: Souza, D. M. (Dorothy M.). Creatures all around us.
QL737.R6S63 1998
599.35'3—dc21   97-5554

Manufactured in the United States of America
1 2 3 4 5 6 – JR – 03 02 01 00 99 98

It's a Mouse!

A house mouse

The room is quiet, except for a faint scratching noise in the far corner. Suddenly a cat pounces, pressing its paw down on a long, gray tail. The furry owner of the tail slips away and races across the room. "Yeek! A mouse!" someone screams.

Outside, a larger mouse with long ears hops under a bush. It sniffs the ground, picks up an acorn with its two front paws, and chomps on the hard shell with its razor-sharp front teeth.

Some hopping mice are found in Australia.

Meanwhile, miles away in a desert, a yellowish brown mouse is standing on its hind legs. Suddenly it begins hopping across the ground like a miniature kangaroo.

Yes, mice are everywhere. They live in a variety of **habitats,** or places. Some, such as house mice, live where we do. Others, such as harvest mice, prefer fields, marshes, and meadows. White-footed mice live in both grasslands and forests. Kangaroo and pocket mice hide in desertlike places, and mice known as lemmings can even be found along the edges of the frozen Arctic. Mice live on every continent except Antarctica.

All mice belong to a large group of animals known as **rodents.** The group includes about two thousand different species (SPEE-sheez), or kinds, of animals. Squirrels, gophers, guinea pigs, beavers, and porcupines are some examples of other rodents. All rodents are part of a larger group of animals called **mammals.** (Humans are part of this group, too.) Mammals have backbones, they have hair covering some or all of their bodies, and they drink their mother's milk when they are young.

Rodents are famous for their habit of gnawing, or chewing, with sharp front teeth. The name "rodent" actually comes from a Latin word that means "to gnaw."

The red squirrel (left) and the beaver (right) are rodents.

This Norwegian rat, a rodent and relative of the mouse, shows its incisors.

Mice and other rodents have four large front teeth called **incisors** (in-SY-zerz). Two are in their upper jaws and two in their lower ones. These teeth are as sharp as a knife and never stop growing. The animals keep their incisors sharp and keep them from getting too long by grinding them together and by gnawing on hard objects.

Rodents also have 8 to 18 grinding teeth, or **molars,** in the back of their mouth. They usually do not have more than 22 teeth in all.

Between the incisors and the molars is an empty space called the **diastema** (dy-uh-STEE-muh). When a rodent is gnawing on something it does not want to swallow, like the shell of a nut, it simply sucks its lips into this space. Then the shell cannot slip down its throat.

6

Mice are the smallest of the rodents. Most have pointed noses, big ears, and skinny, almost hairless, tails. Their coats may be gray, brown, or black, with lighter shades on their undersides. Once in a while, a completely white mouse will be born into a family of gray, brown, or black mice. This white mouse is called an albino.

In the following pages, we'll follow the trails of several different mice. We'll see what they do night and day, how they get together to raise a family, and how they escape the many dangers that surround them.

A harvest mouse grips a branch with its toes.

A Mouse in the House

House mice move indoors when the weather gets cold.

A cool wind blows across a field and makes clouds of dust dance and swirl. A 3-inch house mouse, with a hairless tail almost as long as its body, searches for a warm place to hide. It scurries past a bush and slips through a crack in a building. Then it stops in front of a hole about the size of a penny. The hole leads inside a house. To make sure the opening is large enough for it to wiggle through, the mouse spreads out its whiskers like a fan. The tips of its whiskers barely touch the edges of the hole, so the creature fits through easily.

8

Once on the other side, the mouse sniffs the warm air, trying to catch every scent that floats past it. Since the mouse cannot see more than a few inches away, it uses its nose to discover what its eyes cannot. As it darts ahead, special glands on the bottom of its feet release a strong-smelling liquid. If the creature has to escape in a hurry, it will simply follow the scent of its own tracks.

After exploring a number of dark places, the mouse finds an open drawer full of bags and string. Nearby is a bowl of half-eaten dog food that it can nibble on later. The drawer will be a perfect hideout.

Mice can't see well, so they have to rely on their noses.

Since the mouse is a male, it next begins marking its new **territory,** or the space it will claim as its own. It does this by circling the area and leaving drops of urine as it moves. The smell acts as a warning to other male mice to stay away. One or two females will later be allowed to enter the area, but no males, unless they are members of the mouse's family.

Once the territory has been marked, the house mouse settles down and falls asleep. If a cat or a human does not find it, the mouse will probably stay in its cozy home until the weather outside warms again. Then it may move into a cool basement, a warehouse stocked with food, or some other building where it can find snacks.

Life with humans is full of dangers for a house mouse.

House mice have been living with people and eating their food for thousands of years.

Any animal that shares food and shelter with another species is called a **commensal** (kuh-MEN-suhl). The word means "eating together at the same table." The house mouse doesn't actually sit down and eat with us, but it does live in our homes and other buildings where we have food.

Long ago, house mice, also known as Old World mice, lived only in Europe, Asia, and Africa. When people began to explore other parts of the world, these tiny creatures hid in food supplies on ships and ended up traveling with the explorers. Mice soon began to multiply on every island and continent where explorers landed. In no time, they were living in many different kinds of houses as uninvited guests.

The Wild Ones

A white-footed mouse

A brownish-colored mouse opens its large eyes, stretches, and yawns. It peeks out the entrance of its home in a hollow tree and looks around. The sky is not quite dark enough for it to go seed searching, so it begins grooming itself, or licking the fur all over its body. Carefully, it searches for fleas on its white belly and picks off specks of dirt from between its white toes.

The touches of white on this mouse's body are the reason it is known as a white-footed mouse. This type of mouse is also sometimes called a deer mouse because its coat is almost the same color as a deer's.

Unlike house mice, white-footed mice do not have the habit of living with people. Once in a while, they may move into a summer cabin and hide under a chair, in a box, or even in an old shoe. But most of the time, they set up their homes in hollow trees or stumps or under piles of rocks.

Like many of their relatives, white-footed mice are **nocturnal** (nohk-TUHR-nuhl), that is, they sleep during the day and search for food at night. When it is dark, their **predators** (PREH-duh-tuhrz), or the animals that hunt them, cannot easily spot them.

A white-footed mouse grooms itself with its tongue.

After the white-footed mouse is finished grooming, it races down the trunk of the tree, stops for a moment, and sniffs the air. Nervously, it thumps its long tail on the ground. At any moment, an owl may swoop down on it or a fox may pounce from behind a tree.

Wild mice may live for as long as a year, but they usually live for only two or three months—many animals eat them.

This grasshopper mouse is busy digging a burrow. Notice its stubby tail.

Some distance away in an open field, another mouse, known as a grasshopper mouse, peeks out of its underground burrow. This mouse is cinnamon-colored, although some of its cousins are gray, and it has long ears and a short, thick tail.

Months earlier, the grasshopper mouse dug itself a home using its teeth and feet. A few of its brothers and sisters simply moved into empty burrows that once belonged to gophers or squirrels. But this mouse dug itself a large home. Several tunnels connect rooms that it uses for dining, sleeping, or storing food. It even has one room that it uses as a toilet.

In a nearby meadow of tall grass hangs a small, round nest. It is perched several inches off the ground and has been woven from coarse weed and grass stems. Suddenly, a harvest mouse pops out of a small opening in the nest. This creature looks very much like the house mouse, except that its tail is hairy, not smooth.

While some harvest mice dig burrows as the grasshopper mouse does, many build homes that look like birds' nests. A few even remodel abandoned birds' nests and line them with shredded plant material. The shelters are strong enough to protect the mice from wind and rain.

Most wild mice do not stay outside very long. They nibble and gnaw on whatever they can find, then hurry back to their hideaways. There they groom themselves and take short naps before going out to search for food again.

Harvest mice build their nests in tall grass. They are good climbers.

Mouse Menus

House mice love leftover food.

Mice have big appetites and find a variety of things to eat wherever they go. The house mouse, for example, will feast on dog and cat food. It will sniff along floors, tables, and countertops and inside cupboards, nibbling on crumbs and half-eaten snacks. It will even munch on bars of soap and wallpaper, if nothing else is around.

Like other mice, the house mouse will lap up drops of water now and then. But it can go for long periods without anything to drink. The food it eats contains most of the moisture it needs.

Outside, mice eat seeds, nuts, fruit, and insects. White-footed mice often climb trees in search of some of these treats. Harvest mice run up the stems of weeds and grasses to reach seeds. As the stems bend under their weight, the harvest mice use their tails to balance themselves, much as gymnasts use their arms when walking on a balance beam.

When a grasshopper mouse catches the scent of an insect, one of its favorite foods, its tail shakes excitedly. Its ears twitch as its **prey,** or victim, moves closer. Then the mouse leaps on the insect and sinks its front teeth into the insect's head or neck. Some grasshopper mice eat scorpions and even other mice.

A grasshopper mouse munches on a grasshopper.

A number of mice species store food for winter. Their supply is called a **hoard.** These mice carry seeds, nuts, or roots in their mouths, one or two at a time, and hide them in a variety of places. One hoard may be under a pile of leaves, another in a hollow tree, still another under the ground in the middle of a field. The hoards of one mouse might fill a large grocery bag.

A mouse's hoard in a bird's nest

This pocket mouse has cheeks full of seeds.

Pocket mice gather food for storage much like squirrels do. They have loose pouches, or pockets, on either side of their head. The pockets may reach from the animal's mouth all the way to its shoulders. As pocket mice pick up seeds and nuts and stuff them into their pockets, the pouches stretch and stretch. When their pockets are bulging with food, the mice rush home and empty them. Later, they may clean their pouches by simply turning them inside out.

Many outdoor mice change their diet with the seasons. In spring, when seeds are scarce, they eat insects and buds. In summer, they nibble on roots and fruits. In fall, they feast on nuts, seeds, mushrooms, and fruits, and store the extras in their hoards for winter.

Some jumping mice eat so much in fall they can hardly move. They crawl into underground burrows lined with soft material, curl up in a ball, and **hibernate** (HY-bur-nayt), or fall into a deep sleep. During winter, the jumping mouse does not need to find food. The large supply of food in its body will keep it nourished until spring.

A white-footed mouse (below left) snacks on blackberries, while a striped mouse (below right) nibbles on a cactus.

Nose to Nose

Male house mice fighting outside

Not only does a mouse's sense of smell let the animal know where food is, it also helps the mouse identify other mice. When two mice meet, the first thing they do is try to catch each other's scent.

If a male mouse catches the scent of a strange male in his territory, he will try to chase him away. If he does not succeed, he may bite off the newcomer's whiskers or stand on his hind legs and swat him with his front paws until he leaves.

Two harvest mice, a male and a female, sniff each other.

    Some mice, such as harvest mice, live alone, while others live in small groups. House mice live in groups from time to time. In each group of mice, one male usually becomes the dominant or "top" mouse. Other males try to stay out of his way.

    When females are ready to mate, they give off a special scent. Once a male catches this scent, he will chase the female around. If she stops running, the two will touch noses, then sniff and lick each other.

To attract females, some males show off. The jumping mouse, for example, bounces up and down like a ball. Grasshopper mice chirp and squeak as if singing a song.

After a while, the male mouse climbs on the female's back and deposits his **sperm,** or male cells, inside her. Once the two have mated, the female usually chases the male away so she can begin making a nest for her young.

House mice mating

Raising a Family

A white-footed mouse at its nest

Female house mice make their nests out of anything soft. It may be an old sock that they have chewed into tiny pieces or bits of cotton, paper, or string. Mice that live outside make their nests of grasses, feathers, leaves, or moss. They hide their nests in trees, fallen logs, or underground burrows.

About three weeks after house mice mate, the female gives birth to her **pups,** or babies. A group of pups is called a **litter.** House mice usually have 3 to 11 pups in a litter. Each pup is about the size of a peanut. They are blind and deaf and have pink, hairless, wrinkled skin. This skin is so thin, you can see the mouse's insides.

These baby house mice are one day old.

Baby mice depend on their mother for everything.

The mother stays close to her pups to keep them warm. She licks their bodies and watches so that no harm comes to them. When they are not sleeping, the young mice are sucking milk from the teats, or nipples, on their mother's underside. If an enemy appears, the pups will grab on to these teats and hang on as their mother drags them to safety. Newborn pups are completely helpless. If one is cold, hungry, or uncomfortable, it will cry loudly until someone comes to its rescue.

The male house mouse does not help take care of his young, although he does allow them to stay inside his territory. Male pygmy mice do help with their young, however. If one pup falls off its mother while she is out of the nest, the male pygmy will pick it up in his mouth and bring it home.

Several days after birth, fur begins to appear on the pups. In about two weeks, they are able to see and hear. Their mother chews up bits of food for them to eat, and now and then, she takes them for short walks.

These ten-day-old house mouse babies have fur. Their eyes will open when they are fourteen days old.

A young white-footed mouse explores the world.

When they are about one month old, the young house mice are on their own. In another few weeks, females from the litter are old enough to **breed,** or mate and have babies of their own.

Most female mice have 2 to 7 litters a year, during spring, summer, and sometimes fall. Meadow mice may have as many as 17 litters with seven pups in each. In warm climates and in safe places inside houses, some mice breed all year. Mice in the wild usually live less than a year. If they did not have so many predators, they could outnumber all other creatures on Earth.

On the Run

Mice have many enemies.

Mice must always be on the lookout for enemies. Fortunately, their eyes are on the sides of their heads, so they can spot predators both straight ahead and to the right and left.

A mouse living in your house must beware of dogs, cats, rats, and you. Those living outside must guard against attacks from snakes, weasels, skunks, bobcats, and foxes, as well as owls and hawks. Even mammals as large as bears enjoy a mouse snack now and then.

To avoid being spotted, most mice are well **camouflaged** (KA-muh-flahzhd). This means that their coats blend in with their surroundings and make them almost invisible. Grass mice, for example, have stripes on their back that make them look like blades of grass. Some desert mice have sand-colored fur, and lemmings, which live in the frigid north, turn white during winter to match the snow and ice.

Siberian lemmings (above left), from Russia, turn white to hide in the snow. The fur of the African striped grass mouse (left) helps it to disappear in the grass.

A yellow-necked mouse leaps through the air.

Mice escape many predators because they are small, quick, and nimble. They can dive into a hole, slip under a door, or dart through an opening the size of a dime.

House mice can race up walls, tables, or curtains. They can leap from a shelf to a countertop or from one chair to another in the blink of an eye.

Woodland jumping mice, which weigh less than an ounce, have tiny front legs and large hind ones. They can jump 10 or 12 feet in one hop. If you could jump as well as a woodland jumping mouse can, you would sail more than a mile through the air.

If caught by the tail, some mice are able to free themselves. The Florida mouse, for example, simply sheds part of its tail skin, and its predator ends up with an empty tube of skin in its mouth. The African dormouse has a tail made up of a series of parts. If any one of these parts is caught, it will break off as the dormouse races away. All mice are excellent swimmers and will jump into the water if that is their only escape route.

A few mice escape enemies by being hard to eat. The fur of the spiny mouse is sharp and stiff like a porcupine's. Predators that try to swallow it have a very painful time. They usually don't try to catch a spiny mouse if they spot one again.

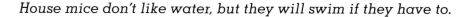

House mice don't like water, but they will swim if they have to.

Sometimes mice warn one another of danger by stamping their feet on the ground or by screaming or whistling. Their squeals are so high-pitched that most creatures cannot hear them. Cats, however, can and often do track their sound. If a mouse is finally cornered, it may stand on its hind legs, put its head in the air, and scream. It does not give up without a fight.

The sharp fur of the Egyptian spiny mouse (above right) helps keep predators away. A grasshopper mouse (right) lets out a high-pitched squeak when another mouse enters its territory.

Mice play an important role in our environment. Each year they destroy thousands of weeds by munching on seeds. They help rid the earth of insect pests. By digging burrows, they keep the soil loose in fields and forests. This allows the roots of plants and trees to grow deeper. Without them, snakes, small mammals, hawks, and owls might have little to eat.

Whether mice are standing on their hind legs, balancing on a blade of grass, munching a seed, or gnawing on a piece of wood, they are fun to watch. So the next time you spot one, try not to scream or run the other way. Stop and watch it for a while. You may end up smiling at what it does.

A yellow-necked mouse rests on a young fern plant.

Mice belong to a group of animals known as rodents. All rodents gnaw with two pairs of sharp front teeth called incisors. Mouselike rodents outnumber all other rodents and live all around the world, except in Antarctica.

Mice that are alike in different ways are grouped together in families. Below are several of these families, a few of the mice that belong to them, and some facts about them.

FAMILY	EXAMPLES	FAVORITE FOODS	NUMBER IN TYPICAL LITTER	HABITAT
Cricetinae	white-footed mouse	seeds, nuts, insects	3-5	woods, farms, prairie
	plains harvest mouse	seeds	2-5	marshes, grassy areas
	grasshopper mouse	insects, other mice	4-5	prairies, deserts
Muridae	house mouse	stored food, plants	3-11	in or near buildings, fields
Heteromyidae	pocket mouse	seeds, greens	2-7	short grass, sandy soil
	kangaroo mouse	seeds	1-7	sandy soil
Kapodidae	jumping mouse	seeds, insects, fruit	2-7	meadows

Glossary

breed: to mate or have young

camouflaged: blended in with one's surroundings

commensal: sharing food with another kind of animal

diastema: the space in a rodent's mouth between its incisors and molars

habitats: the types of places where an animal can live

hibernate: to spend the winter in a hiding place, in a sleeplike state

hoard: a supply of food that is hidden for later use

incisors: the four front teeth of some animals, such as rodents

litter: the group of young that are born to an animal at one time

mammals: animals that are warm-blooded, have a backbone, have hair on their bodies, and feed their young with mother's milk

molars: broad, flat teeth that are used for grinding food

nocturnal: active at night

predators: animals that hunt and eat other animals

prey: an animal that is killed and eaten by other animals

pups: the young of certain animals, such as mice

rodents: a group of animals that gnaw with four continually growing front teeth

sperm: the male cells that fertilize a female's eggs

territory: the area that an animal, such as a mouse, marks as its own

Index

The photographs are reproduced through the courtesy of: © Breck P. Kent, front cover; © Animals Animals/Oxford Scientific Films, back cover; NHPA: pp. 1 (left), 18, 33, 37 (© Stephen Dalton), pp. 7, 9 (© E. A. Janes), p. 17 (© Roger Hosking), p. 20 (© Walter Murray), p. 22 (right) (© Daniel Heuclin), p. 28 (Michael Leach), p. 32 (top) (© Hellio and Van Ingen); © Erwin and Peggy Bauer, pp. 1 (right), 32 (bottom); Aquila Photographics: p. 3 (© Steve Downer), p. 5 (right) (© Wayne Lankinen), p. 10 (© Mike Lane); Animals Animals: p. 4 (© Hans and Judy Beste), pp. 8, 35 (top) (© E. R. Degginger), pp. 12, 14 (© Zig Leszczynski); © Robert McCaw, pp. 5 (left), 26; Ellis Nature Photography/© Michael Durham, pp. 6, 23, 34; Animals Animals/Oxford Scientific Films, p. 11 (© Michael Leach), p. 24 (G. I. Bernard), pp. 25, 27, 29 (Rodger Jackman); © Dwight R. Kuhn, pp. 13, 15, 21, 22 (left); Visuals Unlimited: p. 19 (© William J. Weber), p. 31 (© Joe McDonald), p. 35 (© William Grenfell); © Carolyn Chatterton, p. 30.

J

599.35   Souza, D. M.
S   It's a mouse!

DISCARD

Hiram Halle Memorial Library
Pound Ridge, New York